Be an EXPE...

..in interpretir

Richard Briggs

Scripture Union, 207–209 Queensway, Bletchley, MK2 2EB, England.

First published 1998

ISBN 1 85999 224 2

British Library Cataloguing-in-Publication Data
A catalogue record for this book is available from the British Library.

Cover design by ie Design.
Printed and bound in Great Britain by Creative Print and Design (Wales) Ebbw Vale.

ACKNOWLEDGEMENTS

I have been thinking about biblical interpretation ever since I became a Christian. Back then, a friend suggested that I read the book of Acts, since it was, he assured me, exciting stuff. I got no further than the opening words ('In my former book, Theophilus, I wrote about…') and I was stumped. What former book? Who wrote Acts? I flicked backwards and forwards through my new Bible, checked in the contents page, but got no help. Discouraged, I gave up and went and asked my friend. That sense of exploring God's word with others, and the excitement of discovery, has not stopped since.

So it seems particularly appropriate to acknowledge here the countless conversations with friends, in many different contexts, which have all contributed to the way I think today and which are somehow (however loosely) responsible for this book. In particular I would like to thank Alison Barr, Mark Greene, Mary Moody and others at Scripture Union, who have all offered timely words of encouragement. And a big 'thank you' to Melody, my wife, who not only helped make this book a good deal better than it was when I first wrote it, but who also, several years ago now, was the first person to teach me hermeneutics. I was so impressed, I married her.

Definitions

hermeneutics (n. pl.) 1 An impressive word for 'interpretation'.
2 A particularly impressive word for 'biblical interpretation'. **3** A hopelessly impressive word for 'discussions about the theory of interpretation'.

Hermann Eutics (n. sing.) 1 A German professor specialising in making the Bible complicated.

hermeneutical (adj.) 1 To do with interpretation. **2** That's quite enough definitions. On with the show...

CONTENTS

HOLY BOOK UPDATE

With the release of 'Revelation' here on the Greek Island of Patmos yesterday, it is rumoured that God has brought his so-called 'Holy Book' project to completion. This project has been in progress for hundreds of years now. It has overshot all deadline and budgetary predictions, and required all kinds of technological developments along the way to cope with multiple scrolls, authorship by committee, mass production and the complex legal issues of divine copyright. In all these areas 'Bible' has broken new ground.

In a move that has confounded critics and supporters alike, the closing instalment, 'Revelation', appears to be unlike most of the previous instalments, and religious groups have claimed that it contains material entirely unsuitable for family reading. A spokesperson said, 'The apostle Paul would never have written such sensationalist material.'

Equally controversial is the decision to release 'Bible' without a built-in backup system of 'Help' pages. 'It's hopeless,' said a spokesperson for the church in Rome. 'If this book gets read by just anyone, who knows what it might be taken to mean?' It is widely thought that the Deity will not be taking up his option on issuing an inspired guide to interpreting 'Bible', but commentators expect that a flood of human authors will be filling this gap in centuries to come.

In spite of the clamour for divine clarification on all these issues, God's only comment was reported to be, 'I have nothing further to add.'

Chapter 1

TRUTH, CONTEXT AND OTHER MINOR INTRODUCTORY ISSUES

'Bible Not Handbook for Living' shock claim

God did not write the Bible in English, which most English people believe was just an oversight. More confusingly, he didn't write it as a Handbook for Living. Just think how simple it would be to interpret the Bible if it looked more like this:

> THE BIBLE
> Section 1: God
>   Point 1: God is all-knowing and eternal.
>   Point 2: God created us and God loves us.

And so on right down to:

> Section 5973: Church Car Park Ethics
>   Point 649: But if the pastor has a second car, then only one space should be held in reserve unless points 598 and 603 apply, or it is the day of his MOT test.

Then, of course, we wouldn't have people studying biblical interpretation; we would just have lawyers (and sometimes, in the New Testament, you will notice that these professions did get confused, which didn't help anyone, eg Luke 11:52).

More seriously, we would have a Bible which would be wonderfully relevant for us and totally irrelevant for everyone else who had ever lived. Church car parking wasn't an issue in the Middle Ages, and neither was recycling, nuclear war, which hymn book to use, which denomination to join, whether to shop on a

Sunday, and so on. The idea of a Bible that tried to cover everything which might ever be relevant is simply a non-starter.

So instead we have a Bible that comes to us in a strange form from distant times and faraway places, telling ancient stories and including the letters, old songs and poems people wrote to each other. Which makes it a bit of a failure as a handbook, but much more interesting to read.

The truth, the whole truth, and a lot of other things too

The way the Bible goes about revealing truth, instead of trying to be a handbook of truths, is that it shows us God – or, more particularly, it shows us Jesus. Jesus himself said, 'I am the truth' (John 14:6), which shows that he wasn't using the word 'truth' in the same way we do. We don't think of truth as something that applies to people. But, in the New Testament, the idea of truth is directly linked to ideas like 'faithfulness' or 'keeping your word', which is why Jesus describes himself as truth.

When we turn to the Bible, we do indeed find that one of its major concerns is to reveal truth to us. But in fact God does a whole lot more there than just tell us truths. He makes promises, he offers blessings and even curses, he commands us, he comforts us, he invites us to worship or to praise or to repent or to grieve... And he does almost all of this through stories, letters, poetry or prophecies. So, with the Bible, one of the basic things we have to establish is what kind of writing we are dealing with in any particular Bible passage.

Context(s)

If in doubt, always introduce a technical term! The technical term for 'kind of writing' is *genre*. Two modern examples of genre are 'science fiction' and 'murder mystery'. We are using our knowledge of different genres every time we ask, 'What kind of film shall I get from the video shop this evening?'

Knowing what genre to look for is a particular example of 'reading in context'. We all know the dangers of taking something out of context. With the Bible this is particularly easy to do, since we are talking about a 2,000-year-old book with an unfamiliar background. This means we have to look at the historical and cultural background of different Bible passages, as well as at the various effects these passages have on us. Amongst other things, we will have to think carefully about what the *author* intended, what the *text* itself says and what we, as *readers*, bring to the passage. Becoming an expert in interpreting the Bible is largely a matter of learning how to read it in its various contexts, and these issues will occupy most of our time in this book.

Why bother?

Why bother with all this stuff about how to interpret the Bible? A very good question. There's a lot to be said for just getting on with reading the Bible and not worrying too much about interpretation. But, at the end of the day, it is impossible to read anything unless you have some understanding of its context and background. In fact we are automatically processing background information every time we read the Bible, even if we don't do it very well. In this sense, interpretation itself is not the issue – we all interpret every time we read. However, it is *better* interpretation that we're after.

Here are some less convincing answers to the question 'Why bother?'

1   You normally don't need to interpret the Bible, you just
    have to read it and do what it says – except when you get to
    a difficult or embarrassing bit, and then you need to
    interpret it so that you can show why it doesn't really apply
    to you. So interpretation is for getting round the difficult
    bits and for explaining away all the things you wish God
    hadn't included. Like most of the Old Testament, for
    instance.

2   The reason why we need to learn how to interpret the Bible
    is so that everyone can see why I am right. Everyone else's
    view is just their interpretation.

1270 BC 00:36 PHARAOH'S PALACE STOP PRESS TRANSMISSION P:02

ISRAELITE EXODUS

Public Service Disruption Expected

Further to recent reports of bizarre meteorological conditions and freak events of nature in and around Pharaoh's palace, Egyptian authorities released a terse statement this morning to the effect that Egypt would not be trading on the international money markets today, owing to a sudden and unforeseen domestic labour shortage. Train and bus services are suspended, and all flights in and out of Cairo have been abandoned. Unconfirmed reports suggest that up to 600,000 men plus women and children − nothing less than the entire Israelite slave population − have departed Egypt in an almost unprecedented mass exodus during the night.

Shock waves from this event are already being felt in other centres of empire around the fertile crescent. A spokesperson for the Babylonians announced that security had been stepped up in Babylon, but declined to comment whether the Babylonian government would be attempting to take over the lucrative 'bricks without straw' franchise which, to date, Egypt has monopolised in the Near East.

Other royal palaces have offered condolences to Pharaoh on the death of his son. A state funeral is planned for early next week.

Related News: Pharaoh's office has denied reports that its army suffered a major rout at the Sea of Reeds in the early hours of the morning, claiming that these reports are simply Israelite propaganda. 'This is just another pathetic attempt to distract attention from our good record on interest rates, expansion of the "Nile cruise" business, and pyramid stock flotation,' said a spokesperson for Pharaoh.

3   Spending all our time arguing about how to interpret the Bible is a useful way to avoid having to do what it says.

And finally, the most unanswerable claim of all:

4   Hermeneutics is just a way of avoiding the plain, literal sense of the Bible. (Note that the word 'plain' is very important here: it implies that anyone who can't see it the same way is being deliberately difficult.)

None of these views takes seriously the fact that every time we read we are interpreting. Interpretation is not an optional luxury for those with nothing better to do. Interpretation is the window through which we see the Bible; it is the packaging that always surrounds the passage; it is the loyalty card that rewards regular reading; it is the unseen guest at every Bible study meeting.

Hermeneutics in the Bible itself

Another argument sometimes used against hermeneutics is that it is just a recent development which people used to do perfectly well without. Certainly, people have not always been aware that reading necessarily involves interpretation. But the practice of biblical interpretation goes right back to the Old Testament itself, to Nehemiah chapter 8.

Here the Jews have returned to Jerusalem after being in exile. They have been getting things like walls and taxes sorted out, and have now turned their attention to spiritual matters like having 'quiet times' with God. It falls to Ezra to read to the assembled crowds from the books of the Law. (Ezra was a priest and teacher of the law who had come from Persia to help organise the Jewish people amidst the upheaval of their return to Jerusalem. Although he got a book of the Bible named after him, he actually missed out on most of what happens in it. So he turns up a lot in Nehemiah instead.) Anyway, Ezra reads and the Levites interpret the law for the crowds: 'They gave the sense, so that the people understood the reading' (v 8). From this we learn, among other things, that they didn't find the Old Testament straightforward even when it was being written all around them.

So what do I need?

Here is where we list the tools for the task of biblical interpretation (not including plenty of black coffee, which goes without saying). For some people this is a very short list: it only consists of the Bible, and everything else just complicates matters.

Well, yes, you certainly need a Bible. But the model of 'just me and the Bible' is too individualistic. Perhaps the other most important 'item' on your list is not an obvious one – a friend, or preferably a church full of friends – so that you are not just trying to understand the Bible on your own, regardless of what God is also saying to those around you. Best of all will be a wise friend several steps ahead of you who can help you work things out without always trying to get you to agree with them. With a friend like this you can discuss what you read, explore the various difficult questions that come up and consider how God may be speaking to you through the Bible. And, all the while, they can watch out that you don't start developing weird and wacky ideas such as 'European Monetary Union will be the mark of the Beast' or 'You should believe your church leaders when they tell you to sign away all your money to the church and do whatever they tell you'.

Such a wise friend is, in many ways, a short cut through the jungle of books and reference works available, but a good Bible dictionary, or some commentaries and study guides, can only help. Books also do better than friends when it comes to remembering details over long periods of time.

The final thing on the list is God's help through the Holy Spirit. In John's gospel, Jesus describes the Holy Spirit as our 'advocate' or 'comforter' or 'teacher'. In fact, in the context of John's gospel, 'teacher' is probably the best word for the Holy Spirit since he will lead us into all truth (John 16:13), reminding us of all Jesus taught, and teaching us everything (John 14:26). This puts Jesus at the heart of the Bible and the Spirit at the heart of interpreting it – which is how it should be.

Unfortunately, it also opens the way for that most 'humble' of all claims: 'My interpretation must be right because God told me!' There is no simple way of responding to this. 'Well, God just told me the opposite' is effective but has the considerable disadvantage of not being true. 'If you look at the context, the passage can't possibly mean what you say it means' is often true but sadly not usually effective. So what to do? You could pray, or give them a copy of this book, or perhaps both. When you have read to the end, come back and think about this question again, and see if you have any ideas.

Chapter 2

LEARNING HOW TO READ

Have you ever watched a young child learn to approach different books in different ways? 'My First Book of Road Safety' just doesn't capture the imagination like 'Papa Elephant and the Missing Potty' and requires a whole different set of reading assumptions and skills.

There is no way to break this gently, so here it is: being born again will mean having to learn to read again. At least, if you want to get to grips with the Bible it will. 'My First Book of Tabernacle Dimensions' (Exodus 25–31) also tends not to capture the imagination like 'The Prophets of Baal and the God who Went to the Potty' (for yea, verily and forsooth, 'Your god is on the potty' is a perfectly good translation of part of 1 Kings 18:27).

Here we will look at how to read a passage from the Bible in context – or, in particular, in its historical, literary and biblical contexts. Reading a Bible passage in its proper context is sometimes called *exegesis*, which basically means 'reading out of' the text the meaning which is in it. One way to impress with your expertise here is to remark to someone who has just preached a sermon, 'I appreciated what you said, but I wasn't sure about its exegetical basis.' With a little practice the words 'exegesis' and 'exegetical' can be dropped in all over the place to make it sound like you really know what you are talking about. Try these for size: straightforward exegesis, exegetical foundation, exegetically far-fetched, caffeine-free exegesis...

Exegesis is a major step along the way to interpreting a passage, although it is not the only step. Once you have dug up the meaning of a passage, you might still have a lot of other questions about how it applies to you or how it fits with other passages. These are good questions, but they are not questions about exegesis.

That was then, but this is now

Matthew, Mark and Luke all tell the story of a rich man being told by Jesus to sell his possessions and give to the poor (Matthew 19:16–24; Mark 10:17–25; Luke 18:18–25). The rich man went away furiously trying to think how he could keep his options open on that one. But Jesus was relentless: 'It is easier for a camel to go through the eye of a needle than for someone who is rich to enter the kingdom of God'. After he had finished saying this, Jesus went back to threading his camel on his needle...

Of course, Matthew, Mark and Luke don't include that last sentence, which leaves us wondering just what exactly Jesus did mean. After all, it is plainly impossible to get camels through needles, but most of us know plenty of rich people lining up to enter the kingdom of heaven. What's going on?

This is a perfect situation for a bit of hermeneutical bluffing. Sure enough, around the end of the nineteenth century there began to be reports that there had been, in Bible times, a small gate called 'The Eye of the Needle' which heavy laden camels could only navigate with great difficulty. So what Jesus was saying is how difficult it is to enter the kingdom while carrying all your riches with you. He wasn't talking about impossibility at all. What a relief...

However, there turned out to be no evidence for this 'Eye of the Needle' gate. There never had been any such thing. Jesus really had meant all along that trusting in your own merits to get you into heaven is simply impossible.

What does all this show? That background information affects our understanding. If there had been a gate, it would have altered our perception of the passage's meaning. In general, we need historical information to help us make sure that we are dealing with the passage on its own terms. In other words, that was then, but this is now and an awful lot has changed. This is the issue of *historical context*. It isn't the only type of context around, but it is one of the most basic.

How do I know what it's saying to me?

Reading the Bible in its historical context gets a lot of bad press in the church, and it's easy to see why. It's harder than reading it out of context. It usually involves a bit of background work. And it will always trip up people whose idea of preparing a sermon is to read the passage through a couple of times in the car on the way to the service (no matter how passionately they may pray for wisdom). It's so much easier to say, 'God is telling us to have a collection every week to raise money for the church, just as Paul said in 1 Corinthians 16:1', than to say, 'Paul told the Corinthians to set aside money for a special collection for the struggling churches in Jerusalem, and from this we can understand some biblical priorities about giving...'

Of course, you can only get away with bypassing the historical context in certain kinds of passages. Consider verse 10 of the same chapter: 'If Timothy comes, see that he has nothing to fear among you...' You would soon find yourself in a tangle if you tried to preach a message along the lines of 'God is telling us to be prepared to look after Timothy': this verse is obviously not written for us. How, then, can you tell whether a passage is aimed at you?

A popular view is that if the passage will inconvenience you, then it is not for you. People who adopt this answer have a good deal of tradition on their side.

Others say that it is the principles which count and the details are not too important. There is something in this, but it still does not mean we can avoid the questions of historical context or we could miss the principles altogether. As in the following example.

Who's wearing the trousers?

Consider the following quote from the good book: 'A woman must not wear men's clothing, nor a man wear women's clothing, for the Lord your God detests anyone who does this' (Deuteronomy 22:5, *NIV*). There are all kinds of reasons why you might want to think twice about this verse, especially if you happen to be a woman wearing trousers when you read it.

Of course, trousers are not just 'men's clothing' these days; but they used to be, say, a hundred years ago. So you could try arguing that God, like pretty much everyone else, has simply gone with the latest fashions; he used to find this kind of thing detestable but he doesn't really mind any more. Doesn't sound like there's much mileage in that, does there?

Alternatively, you could argue that it was important then (whenever 'then' was), but today it doesn't matter. Now this may be true, but the verse doesn't actually talk about what is culturally acceptable, only what God finds detestable. So this argument turns out to be just a long-range version of the first one.

If you're really ambitious, you could say that this verse was part of Old Testament law, but we don't live under the law any more – a good example of how to jump out of the frying pan and into the fire, which people do a lot with biblical interpretation. At least here there is no need to have a whole theory of how the Old Testament relates to us today before we can deal with this one verse. Just as well, actually, since the question of how much of the Old Testament relates to us today is a tricky one and, in practice, very few Christians want to throw out all of it. This usually leaves them looking for reasons to throw out some bits and not others, all of which leads to some rotten hermeneutics.

The problem with all of these approaches is that they are not stopping to ask about the historical background to the verse before jumping in and assuming that we know exactly what it is talking about. In fact when Deuteronomy 22:5 talks about 'clothing', it is most likely referring to garments (or even just 'things') worn for magical rites. Probably this verse was forbidding the performance of magic as part of a fertility ritual for couples who wanted a child. God was sure to find magic practices like that detestable because they basically involved praying to another god.

Perhaps you should have been suspicious right at the start of this example. After all, it involved just one sentence plucked out of thin air and giving you no idea of its context in Deuteronomy chapter 22. Consider the following sentence taken out of context from a recipe book: 'Beat until stiff and then stand in the fridge'. You can

---

AD 56 00:48 CORINTH   STOP PRESS TRANSMISSION P:03

GOD CONDEMNS ALL RESTAURANTS

In a shock announcement today God has forbidden all people everywhere to eat in restaurants. He clearly states, in Paul's new letter to the Corinthians, that 'If anyone is hungry, he should eat at home' (I Corinthians 11:34).

'This is a tremendous victory for us,' said a spokesperson for the Christians Against Fast Food Coalition, 'although we had hoped that it would only apply to fast food chains.' Angry restaurant managers have claimed that this is just another example of Christian narrow-mindedness, and some have pointed out that there is nothing in the passage to prohibit women from eating out. Some have even claimed that the relevant passage only prohibits hungry people from eating out, but that light snackers may be exempted.

The apostle Paul is no stranger to controversy. His statement to the Roman Christians that a man whose faith is weak eats only vegetables (Romans 14:2) resulted in lengthy court-cases involving the Vegetarian Wholefood Association and European cattle farmers. He was unavailable for comment last night since he was at a party thrown for him by the International Christian Hat-Makers Society, who are rumoured to have funded the publication of I Corinthians.

---

be sure that if this were a sentence from the Bible, someone somewhere would be trying to get a three-point sermon out of it.

It all depends on how you tell it...

'Once upon a time there was a beautiful princess who lived with her ageing father in a castle on the top of a hill...'

These words clue you in automatically to the fact that you are about to read a fairy tale and that asking questions like 'What was the constitutional status of the monarchy in this country?' or 'What did it mean in that culture to be beautiful?' will not help you much in understanding the story.

Sadly, we don't have time to get into a fairy tale right now, so here's a biblical story instead: '*A man was going down from Jerusalem to Jericho, and fell into the hands of robbers...*'

This is the parable of the Good Samaritan from Luke chapter 10, and once again we should find ourselves automatically aware that this is a story: we don't need to be asking how long the journey was or whether he was heading south or north. The road from Jerusalem to Jericho was a steep and difficult one, and the journey was well-known for being dangerous as it cut through remote mountain passes. But whether this helps you much in understanding the parable is debatable.

Picking up these kinds of clues about what you are reading is called 'being sensitive to the *literary context* of the passage'. Often a few words is all it takes. Look at the opening words in both Genesis and John: 'In the beginning...' Obviously here we are talking wide-screen big-picture stuff. The contrast between the beginning of John's gospel and that of the other three is particularly striking. John is painting with big broad theological brushstrokes, whereas Luke, for instance, is telling us who did what and when. The different openings invite us to take a different approach to each gospel. By way of contrast, anyone starting 1 Chronicles will immediately detect that they are not browsing through the best-sellers section of the Bible.

Literary context is important. Becoming good at spotting different kinds of literary context is known as *literary competence*. This means not reading a parable as if it were history, or a poem as if it were scientific description. Literary competence is a skill, not a process, and who we are makes a difference. Some people have pointed out the similarity between being sensitive to the passage we are reading and being sensitive to a person we are talking to. If we are good listeners – willing to let others explain their ideas in their own way without interrupting or assuming we know what they will say before they say it – then we are also likely to be good readers, open to the particular concerns and ideas of a passage. This has a lot to do with being patient, gentle and caring enough to make sure we understand correctly what is being said.

AD 90 01:03 JERUSALEM   STOP PRESS TRANSMISSION P:04

NEW GOSPEL TEXT FOUND

Great excitement here in Jerusalem yesterday at the announcement that a new gospel text has been discovered amongst the recently released collected papers of the apostle John. It is said to concern a story about a woman found committing adultery and Jesus' response to those who wanted to stone her. The story has been known in oral tradition for many years but has puzzled Christians by not turning up in any of the published gospels. With rumours growing that there will be no fifth gospel to go with the four we already have, and with Thomas allegedly way behind on his own gospel project, it had been thought that the story of the woman in adultery would not make it into the Bible.

However, sources close to John's literary estate announced yesterday that amongst his papers was this small fragment with 'This bit inspired' scribbled in the margin. There is some debate about where this new text fits with the existing gospel. Some have suggested that it should appear just before the 'light of the world' section. It is thought unlikely that it will remain as a separate fifth gospel when the completed New Testament is released, an event which is expected in the relatively near future.

Meanwhile, the search goes on for the lost ending of Mark's gospel, thought to have been lost when the scribe who was copying it died from a snake bite.

And, since these characteristics are all to do with the work of the Holy Spirit in our lives, there is a good case to be made that our spiritual sensitivity plays a part in how well we can read the Bible – which is a good example of how we need God's help in biblical interpretation.

It's all in the good book

'An eye for an eye and a tooth for a tooth', but later 'turn the other

cheek'! With this so-called contradiction many people have
delighted in 'proving' that the Bible doesn't make any sense. It
was Jesus, of course, who first took this Old Testament verse
(Deuteronomy 19:21) and, in the Sermon on the Mount (Matthew
5:38–39), contrasted it with his own teaching. So, was he contra-
dicting the Old Testament? Not at all, but we will have to understand two different contexts to be clear about this.

First, we need the *historical context* of the verse taken from the
Old Testament law. 'An eye for an eye' was part of the Israelite
attempt to bring in a fairer judicial system at a time when, for
instance, stealing one sheep could lead to the wholesale destruc-
tion of the thief's family and property in revenge. The 'eye for an
eye' principle attempted to limit that kind of overkill (eg Leviticus
24:19–20, one of the three places where the principle occurs).

We also need to look at the *biblical context* of Jesus' teaching
to see what he is doing. The Sermon on the Mount (Matthew 5–7)
is where he claims that he is fulfilling the Jewish law himself
(5:17–20): in the same way that the prophets pointed to him as the
Messiah, so also the Law pointed to him as the one who would
live the perfect life that God required. As the Israelite law tried to
set new standards of behaviour, so Jesus is doing the same.

Biblical context includes things like historical background and
literary style, but it also takes seriously the way the Bible functions
as one complete, inspired book. Often the 'context' that matters
most is how the passage relates to other biblical texts. The above
example about the relationship between the Old Testament law and
the New Testament 'gospel' is a difficult one, but it is a clear case
of the need to see how each verse and passage fits into the bigger
picture of the whole Bible. The phrase *canonical context* is sometimes used to talk of this kind of context. The canon is the defini-
tive list of books in the Bible drawn up by the early church to settle
debates about what counted as inspired scripture and what didn't.
(The fact that these have been noisy and sometimes explosive
debates down through the centuries has nothing to do with this list
being called a canon.) Later, we will come across an example of
the importance of this kind of context in Psalm 1.

Chapter 3

THE I-SPY BOOK OF BIBLICAL GENRES

Having looked at historical, literary and biblical contexts, it is time to get down to some specifics and see what the different 'kinds of writings' (genres) we find in the Bible actually look like. So welcome to this all-new, patent-pending, I-spy book of biblical genres. Score one point for each genre you find, and two if you can find one that's not in this list. We will start with things that look like stories, then move on to things that don't.

History

History is such a broad category, it is almost useless as a genre identification. Nevertheless, for many people this is the biggie since *if it ain't history, it ain't true*. This is not a good approach, because it confuses whether something *is* historical (experts like to call this *historicity*) with whether something *is trying to be* historical in the first place.

For example, suppose someone wrote the book of Jonah as a story, to make a point – a bit like a parable in fact. Then the fact that it hadn't happened would have nothing to do with its truth. This is a classic case of getting into muddles with genres. 'Did it actually happen?' may not always be the most helpful question to ask. In the case of Jonah, we don't actually know whether someone wrote a story or whether they tried to write down what happened to the real, historical Jonah. So, you might think, there's not much point in wasting time on that question. But for some people this appears to be a much more pressing issue than 'What is God like?' or 'What does it mean to offer ourselves as living sacrifices to him?', and the historical and biological possibilities of big fish swallowing whole people become a major part of proving the credibility of Christianity...

Narratives and stories

A slightly more useful term is *narrative*, which simply refers to any section of literature written to tell (or narrate) a story. *Historical narrative* is a subset of narrative in general, where the story being told reports something which happened. Another kind of narrative is *mythical narrative*. Defined positively, this refers to any great ancient story that tries to explain the way the world is or was. Defined negatively, it is 'a bunch of mystical hocus-pocus', like the world floating on a giant turtle or angry gods hurling mountains at each other. You should probably try to avoid confusing these two definitions. Mythical beasts and warring deities don't feature very heavily in the Old Testament, a characteristic that sets it apart from similar writings of its time. However, fans of talking donkeys should check out Numbers chapter 22.

Since much of the time we do not really know whether or not the narrative is trying to report something that happened, these days the word 'story' is used as an alternative in the whole debate about history. 'Story' in this sense has become, believe it or not, a technical word meaning 'a narrative which may or may not be historical, but it doesn't matter anyway'. It doesn't matter because the powerful thing about a story is the way it captures your imagination and 'speaks to you', not what it tells you about the past. Is this development a good thing?

It is important always to answer a question like 'Is this a good thing?' by saying, 'Well, yes and no. It all depends on what we mean exactly.' The word 'story' is not helpful if it means that we lose sight of the historical basis of the Christian faith, in the life and death and resurrection of Jesus. The stories told about him in the gospels are trying to show, at least in part, what really happened. If it is just a story, and never happened, then this makes a difference. (Note that in cases like this, where it matters, it has always turned out, on investigation, that the Bible is historically reliable, sometimes even down to minor details.)

But, on the other hand, focusing on the story can be a good thing. Sometimes we have little idea of the literary context, and we don't have a clue whether the story really 'happened': there is simply no evidence either way. In such cases, no one can say for sure whether it is the story or the history behind the story that matters. Books like Job and Esther fall into this category: Esther has a historical setting, but then so does *War and Peace*. The best way forward is not to worry about historicity too much, but to get on with enjoying the stories.

Gospels

Still on things that look like stories, there has been some debate about what a *gospel* actually is. Is it a biography? Is it historical or literary, or both? Is it a unique kind of writing that we only find in the Bible?

A few years ago the experts were generally going for the last option: we only have gospels in the Bible and there is really nothing like them. So everyone learned that gospels were not biographies: they didn't, for example, record the whole life of Jesus, and they were organised around theological themes. Then the wind changed and it is now much more fashionable to believe that the gospels are biographies again. Not like modern ones, of course, but nevertheless a lot like your average Greco-Roman biography. The chances of anyone catching you out by having a better knowledge of Greco-Roman biography than you do are, let's face it, pretty slim, so you can afford to sound fairly confident with this one.

Some people like to distinguish between John's gospel and the other three which are known as 'the synoptic gospels'. This has nothing to do with the fact that it is impossible to provide a synopsis of, say, Luke or Mark which is any shorter than the gospel itself, and has everything to do with the fact that 'synoptic' means 'seen together'. These three gospels cut and paste the same material in different orders. In other words, they all look at basically the same stories – they 'see them together' – hence the name 'synoptic gospel'. John, on the other hand, tends to stick with altogether different stories. On the rare occasions when he does refer to an incident from the synoptic gospels, such as the feeding of the five thousand, scholars have been known to call this an 'optical allusion'.

Parables

Parables, which occur mainly in the gospels, are little riddles or stories told to make people think. Jesus used this teaching device a lot. Understanding a parable is a bit like getting a joke: you have to 'get the point' to see why it was told. This 'getting the point' is sometimes known technically as a 'gestalt moment', or less technically as an 'A-ha! moment', since when you get the point you usually say something like 'A-ha!' Whatever you call it, this is an important point in hermeneutics and we will come back to it later.

Not long ago it was fashionable to say that a parable could have only one point. This was a neat theory which did away with a lot of funny ideas about reading the parables as allegories. An *allegory* is where everything in the parable stands for something else, so that, for instance, the two coins in the parable of the Good Samaritan could represent the sacraments (!), or the two Testaments, or the law and the gospel, or any other of the immediately obvious things that come to mind when you hear 'two coins'. So the 'only one point' argument seemed to tidy things up nicely – until people realised there was no evidence for it. For example, the parable of the two sons in Luke chapter 15 makes at least two points, depending on which son you identify with. So that's another well-established idea everyone now tries to pretend they never believed...

The 'We' passages

One other type of narrative worth mentioning is the famous 'We' passages in Acts (16:10–17; 20:5 – 21:18; 27:1 – 28:16). These unusual passages, written in the first person plural, are very short and were discovered by a Scotsman, hence their name. More to the point, the fact that they represent an eye-witness account by someone who was there tends to provide yet more evidence, if it is needed, that the New Testament (and, in particular, the book of Acts) tells it like it was. The phrase that should trip off your tongue at this point is 'Good indication of historical reliability'.

Letters

What is the Bible doing when it's not telling stories? Well, in the New Testament what it does is give us *epistles*, which is the experts' term for letters. Epistles should not be confused with apostles, who were the people who wrote them. Usually we only get one side of the correspondence on these occasions, so it is a bit like listening to one end of a telephone conversation. But 'half a telephone conversation' has not yet caught on as a genre description.

Epistles come with a whole set of subdivisions which make up genres in themselves. These include:

Standardised introductions, rather like 'To:
church.god@corinth.com'.

Further introductory thanksgiving, except, most
noticeably, in Galatians 1:6 – a pretty big clue that
when Paul wrote to the Galatians he was extremely
annoyed with them.

Paraenesis – the experts' term for the bit of the letter which
takes all the theological discussion and turns it into
practical advice (and usually begins with a great big
'THEREFORE', eg Romans 12:1).

Concluding exhortations, the strangest of which is the last
verse of 1 John – this is hardly a conclusion at all, but
appears to be another section of the letter John simply
never got round to writing (although it may be that we
are just not very familiar with all the different styles of
first century letters!).

Apocalyptic

Despite its name, *apocalyptic* is not a style of pre-Caribbean rhythmic singalong, but a picturesque 'Mark-my-words-there'll-be trouble-ahead' kind of language. The Bible tends to use this at moments of extreme unease with the way the world is, eg in Revelation, or the second half of the book of Daniel after they ran out of Sunday School stories. An alternative theory is that the

Bible uses this genre at times when the author had eaten something that disagreed with him, which is why he wrote stuff nobody could understand.

Apocalyptic should not be confused with the apocrypha, a highly varied collection of books, mainly from the period between the Old and New Testaments, which tell Jewish and early Christian stories, report on prophecies, and offer wisdom and advice (a bit like Proverbs). The apocrypha can often be distinguished from the Bible by phenomena such as angels carrying prophets around or mysterious hidden scrolls revealing everything in numbers. As you can tell from this description, the same style of writing is still popular at station bookstalls today.

Old Testament genres

The Old Testament has a whole variety of genres besides the narrative parts. The most charming is the existential angst of Ecclesiastes. 'Existential angst' is not a technical description of a genre but, rather, a tremendously impressive term for the way some people get so uptight about life, they dress in black, get trendy haircuts and spend all their time sitting in cafés wondering why they exist. It is a fairly accurate description of Ecclesiastes, although we can't actually prove that this book was written in a café. Ecclesiastes begins with the startling claim, 'Meaningless, meaningless, utterly meaningless! Everything is meaningless.' Anyone trying to ignore the context of this verse and construct a three-point sermon based on it will soon be found out.

More generally, we have *poetry*, particularly the psalms, which turn upside down the notion of God speaking to his people through the Bible, since they are composed entirely of God's people speaking to God. The historical context of the psalms is almost impossible to know. Although some of them come with handy titles like 'Written by David when he had a flat tyre in the wilderness of En Gedi', these are really guesses (sometimes good guesses, admittedly) which were added later, long after the psalm had first come into circulation.

One of the longest poems in the Bible is the Song of Songs, which is mainly about how wonderful sex is. Many people have found it impossible to believe that the Bible would ever say this and so claim that this poem is actually about Christ and the Church. However, to get away with this, they really need to argue convincingly that the canonical context of a book overrules all the other contexts, and that is certainly debatable. More likely, the poem works both as a lover's song and as an image of the relationship between God and his people (such as is used in, for instance, Jeremiah 2:2).

Alternatively, of course, you could just enjoy what it says about sex.

The proverbs are the clearest example of *wisdom literature*. They were usually short and memorable sayings composed by after-dinner speakers in the royal court of Solomon, many of whom appear to have had rather interesting experiences of marriage, hence the frequent references to wives as dripping taps or leaky roofs. The picture of the perfect wife in Proverbs 31 – who is not only beautiful, widely respected, a devoted mother and a wise teacher, but who also manages to make a profit before breakfast – perhaps also indicates some wishful male thinking. The perfect husband, by way of contrast, is conspicuous by his absence.

Prophecy plays a major role in the Old Testament canon. Most of what we call 'the prophetic books' (eg Isaiah, Jeremiah) are made up of *prophetic oracles*, which were shorter sayings given on various occasions and edited together into the longer books we now have. This is why some of them are difficult to read through in one go. The person who edited together a book like Isaiah is called 'a redactor'. The person who reads an entire book like Isaiah straight through is called 'tired'.

When the Jews put their canon together, the first books that they called prophecy were Samuel and Kings, which we call history – further proof that classifying books by genre is a tricky business.

Two other common genres are *legal codes* (like much of Leviticus and Deuteronomy) and *genealogies* (lists of family and clan names) which turn up in all kinds of places, eg the very first chapter of the New Testament. These two genres were included by people who were worried that if reading the Bible was made too entertaining then folk would stop believing it was good for them.

For the advanced genre spotter

Most of the genres listed above are fairly easy to recognise. But as a reminder that the Bible comes to us from an unfamiliar background, we will discover on closer inspection that there are

---

550 BC 01:14 JERUSALEM   STOP PRESS TRANSMISSION P:05

EVERYDAY WITH LEVITICUS

Stuck when your friends ask you about the regulations for mildew? Need help understanding the difference between clean and unclean animals?

The publishers of the highly popular 'Build Your Own Model Tabernacle in 24 Days' are proud to introduce 'Everyday with Leviticus – a Guide to Daily Living'.

Leviticus speaks powerfully into our daily needs. Be stimulated to a greater awareness of who God is, and what he requires of us. Thrill to the immediacy and challenge of the text. Its pages will grip you with terrifying intensity as you discover the astonishing perfection of God's holiness, explore the practical issues surrounding morality and ethics, and see the wonder of God's provision of atonement for us.

Also included:

• A cut-out-and-keep wall-chart on the regulations governing infectious skin diseases
• Background to that controversial verse which states that when a man has lost his hair and is bald, then he is clean (Leviticus 13:40).

'Everyday with Leviticus' is available at a festival near you. Coming soon: 'Through Hezekiah's Tunnel in Six Daily Readings'.

---

various other recurring patterns in scripture. Score extra points if you recognise any of the following.

Annunciation scenes typically feature an angel appearing in blinding glory with an urgent post-paid message from above. *Household codes* are lists of rules for family living (eg Colossians 3:18 – 4:1). *Lists of virtues and vices* (eg Ephesians 4:31–32) are a standard ancient way of contrasting different lifestyles – although you often only get the virtues or the vices separately, depending on the mood of the writer. In *prophetic commissioning scenes*, a prophet discovers a job description sent from on high and spies trouble ahead (eg Exodus 3 or Isaiah 6).

Perhaps the most fascinating of all genres is the 'man meets woman at well' *romantic episode*. Isaac, Jacob and Moses all find wives this way (see Genesis 24,29; Exodus 2). Thus when Jesus meets the Samaritan woman at the well, in John chapter 4, the stage is set for a wedding … or is it? In terms of genre, it is startling that Jesus doesn't marry the woman; in terms of the society of the time, it would have been shocking if he had. And, as a result of this tension, readers of the story are left wondering what Jesus will actually do. In a scene where gender and racial boundaries are challenged time and again, he invites her into an eternal relationship with God. As the apostle Paul might say, she becomes part of the bride of Christ…

How to take care of your genre collection

After you have patiently spotted all these different genres, you may be wondering what to do with them. The important thing is to use them and not let them sit around getting rusty.

There is a famous song, sometimes thought to go back to Moses, which begins 'Read your Bible, pray every day…' (but Moses sang it in Hebrew). From this has come the notion of The Quiet Time. The Quiet Time is that period of the day when a Christian sits down for a few minutes and quietly reflects on the fact that they haven't read the Bible for ages. They then open the Bible, read some of it, and pray.

There is always a danger in this approach that you end up reading out of context. If your quiet time consists of opening the Bible at Leviticus 3:16 and reading, 'All fat is the Lord's', this one verse might prompt you to lead a devotional talk at the next meeting of your local Christian Slimmers' Association. Alas, you will certainly be missing the point. However, if you read John 3:16 and talked about our need for God, or 2 Timothy 3:16 and talked about the authority of the Bible, you might get away with it. Why?

The answer is that passages in the gospels or letters may communicate important messages in just a few words, whereas with narratives (or, in our example, legal codes) you need a longer passage to get the point. So taking care of your genre collection is a matter of practical importance. 'What God is saying to me' through any passage will be said in different ways depending on the genre of the passage. As a basic rule of thumb, to understand a parable, a prophecy or a proverb, read the whole thing (they are all usually short, so this is not normally a problem). However, to understand a story, read the whole thing though it may take a lot longer, as the following example demonstrates.

Gideon: The founding father of fleeces?

Gideon's story is told in Judges chapters 6–8, where he is described as 'a mighty warrior' by an angel who possibly had his tongue firmly in his cheek (Judges 6:12). Unsure whether God is really going to use him to deliver Israel, Gideon asks for a sign from God to confirm his divine intentions. Can God make Gideon's woollen fleece wet and the ground dry overnight? Yes, he can. So Gideon asks for the reverse as a second sign. And God obliges.

Thus began a long tradition – which would astonish Gideon if he knew of it – of 'laying a fleece before the Lord' to test out what he wants. Since most modern Westerners do not have a handy supply of fleeces, they often take this metaphorically and say things like, 'God, if you want me to give money to the poor this Christmas, then please double my income first.'

Budding experts will by now be able to spot the 'hermeneutical leap' (as we say in the trade) that was made from the Bible story to the tradition. Not everything that happens in biblical narrative is a model for us. Later, in the book of Judges, a short-sighted judge promises to sacrifice to the Lord the first living thing he sees on returning home from battle, only to find that it is his daughter (Judges 11:29–40). Unsurprisingly, our hermeneutical muscles are rapidly stretched to the limit at the prospect of applying this awful story to ourselves. Instead we conclude, rightly, that here is a classic example of what not to do. So the obvious question is, how can we tell whether Gideon's fleece is an example of what to do or what not to do? Perhaps it is neither. Perhaps it is just a record of what Gideon did.

How can narrative tell us anything? Probably not in short sound bites, but over longer passages where you get the big picture about what is and isn't a good idea. And the big picture painted in Judges is this: Gideon, like most of the so-called 'heroes' in the book, is simply one more person God used, in spite of their weaknesses, to do great things. So the narrative tells us lots of things; perhaps especially that God will use us despite our failings.

But it does not teach us to lay fleeces.

Now if this isn't the right interpretation, then, when you wake up in the morning, may this book be wet and all the books around it dry…

How long is a long story?

Genesis is a tremendous story, with a great deal to tell us. However, to get it in focus we need to read all fifty chapters. If we focus on individual words or sentences too much, we will find all kinds of things God didn't intend to say – rather like the preachers who enjoy telling you all about the significance of the badger skins in the tabernacle in Exodus, but who neglect to mention the event of the exodus itself with all its social and political implications.

Is reading the whole of a book like Genesis enough to settle any questions of interpretation it raises? As a story, Genesis doesn't have a very satisfactory ending. This is because it runs right on into Exodus and then goes on to make up the Pentateuch (the five books of Moses). In turn, the Pentateuch becomes part of what is called the Primary History, so called because it is a history and, well, because it comes before everything else. This takes us as far as the end of 2 Kings. By this time you can see it coming – the best context of all for reading Genesis is to read it as a part of the whole Bible, seeing how it fits with everything else God has chosen to say.

Therefore, what God is saying through Genesis all depends on how you look at it. And, in principle, he could be saying a lot of different things depending on the context in which you are reading. He could be revealing the beginnings of Israel; the story of why the world is in a mess and what he proposes to do about it; the historical background to the Law; or how he works with such unpromising material as Abraham, Isaac, Jacob, Joseph and others, giving us hope that maybe he can even work through us. He is definitely not revealing where you should look for the ark, how to pretend to be your brother so that you can get your father's blessing, how to lie about your wife being your sister, or how to laugh at angels.

Why, the hermeneutical implications alone are staggering...

Chapter 4

HOW TO GET THERE FROM HERE

There is a well-known story about the man who was driving along one day and realised he was lost. Pulling over, he stopped a pedestrian and asked how to get to where he was going. The pedestrian thought carefully and said, 'Well, you can't get there from here.'

The feeling that you can't get there from here is a familiar one for some Bible readers. How can my world relate to the world of the Bible? On the face of it, it is an uneven match. In the blue corner is the Bible, the world's most read and most famous book, which has spoken to humankind down through centuries. It concerns itself with the great themes of God – creation, redemption, sin, suffering, good and evil, and the history of the world (at least, a large chunk of the ancient world). Meanwhile, you are in the red corner. Right now your world is concerned with things like finding a parking space, affording your weekly food, passing an upcoming exam, falling in love, coping with a baby who won't sleep at nights, trying to find a job... You would dearly like God to speak to you on these issues, but whenever you read the Bible it appears to be preoccupied with these other matters.

The question of how to bridge the gap between what was going on back then and what is happening to you now is perhaps *the* major concern of hermeneutics. In looking at the questions of reading in context and understanding different genres, we have really only been thinking about 'back then'. Now we need to see how it might relate to our own lives today.

What does it all mean?
We can make a start on this task of bridging the gap by looking at

how we discover the meaning of a Bible passage in practice.

There are three places to look for the meaning of a Bible passage. (Not counting those study Bibles that come with extra notes printed at the bottom of the page which give you the 'answers'. You might find the meaning there of course!) The meaning of a passage, basically, depends on what the author wanted to say, what the words and sentences in the passage mean, and what the reader understands as he reads. Indeed, it usually requires a bit of negotiation between these three things – author, text and reader. Unfortunately, it is not quite as simple as 'just add water and mix', so we will take them one at a time and see how they all contribute to the meaning.

Inside the mind of the author

One of the important questions about the meaning of a text is, what did the author mean, or intend, when he wrote it? Authorial intention is a key ingredient in understanding the Bible.

For some people the meaning of, say, Romans 1:16–17 is whatever Paul had in mind when he wrote, 'I am not ashamed of the gospel; it is the power of God for salvation to everyone who has faith...' This is definitely a good approach, although it may need tightening up since Paul could have been thinking of all sorts of things as he wrote. Perhaps he was wondering whether he would finish the letter in time to make the last post; what he was going to say in next Saturday's sermon; maybe even when he was going to stop feeling sick from the eggs he had for breakfast. Paul may have had all these things in mind, but they don't have much to do with the meaning of Romans 1:16–17. However, by and large, it is always worthwhile to ask what the author had in mind when he wrote, or, more exactly, what he intended to say.

One advantage of this approach is that it cuts out a lot of weird and wacky interpretations which rely on ideas like the author of Revelation knowing all about the Gulf War, or Moses having an opinion on the National Lottery. A disadvantage is that it appears to leave you and the Bible back in your opposing corners, not really on speaking terms when it comes to the modern-day issues you are facing. So what other ways in might there be?

Meanwhile, back at the text

The belief that the meaning of a passage is linked to what the author was trying to express is sometimes known as *romanticism*. At the opposite end of the scale, for the less romantically inclined, we find *structuralism*. Now this is an extremely impressive word to learn since virtually nobody knows what it means. In fact the only people who ever did understand it wrote books on it, and there were only a couple of them, making it one of the least widely believed 'isms' of all time. Basically, when you boil it down to practical issues, structuralists say it's not what the author thinks that matters but what the text actually says.

You may be thinking that there is not a lot of difference between what the author thinks and what the text says, but there turns out to be a fair amount of difference. A lot of things an author wants to say he doesn't come out and say explicitly; you have to read them between the lines. A lot of the things we understand about the Trinity, for example, can only be read between the lines in the Bible, which makes hardly any clear statements about the Trinity. As another example, a structuralist would have a difficulty with the theory we mentioned earlier, that the Song of Songs is all about Christ and the church. A romanticist, however, would be happier with it (which just goes to show that romanticism and romance are not the same things at all).

Even combining the author and the text, we still find that the bridge between now and 'back then', between us and the Bible, is a shaky one. You may find that the Bible has a lot to say about relationships, for example, but what you want is for it to say something about *your* relationships. How can it do that? There is one obvious part of the picture still missing – the reader, you yourself.

The reader responds

The bridge between here and there, between now and then, becomes crossable when we realise that we are part of the Bible's message. The Bible is communicating with us, and we play a part in making that communication happen every time we read it. This is part of the reason why we never reach the point in the Christian life of saying, 'Well, I've read the Bible now, so what next?' There is always more, because every time we read the biblical text it communicates with us in a new way.

AD 75 01:33 ROME   STOP PRESS TRANSMISSION P:06

NEW SECTION OF LUKE'S GOSPEL RELEASED

Work continues on Luke's gospel here in Rome. Luke released his trial text yesterday for what is projected to be the beginning of chapter 15. Text as follows:

Now all the double-glazing telesales people and drug addicts were hanging around Jesus wherever he spoke. And the Christians, especially the ones who studied the Bible a lot, were getting fed up with this, and saying, 'This fellow welcomes druggies and even goes down the pub with them.' So he told them this story. 'Which one of you, having a hundred clients and losing one of them, doesn't leave the ninety-nine on hold and go after the one that is lost until you get a new deal? And when you have signed the contract, you take it home rejoicing. You call together your friends and neighbours, saying to them, "Have a drink with me, for I have re-negotiated the deal we lost." In the same way, mate, there will be more joy in heaven over one drug addict who sorts himself out and makes a few changes to his life than over ninety-nine Christians who don't need to change.

'Or what teenage girl, having a complete set of Spice Girl earrings, if she loses one of them, doesn't turn off the stereo, turn up the lights, and pull her bedroom apart until she finds it? When she has found it she calls her best friend on the phone and tells her the whole traumatic story, and they go out and buy another poster to celebrate. In the same way, mate, the angels are turning up the celestial stereo every time someone sees the light.'

Most people who read the Bible have one very good question in mind, 'What does this mean to me?' And indeed, some people have argued that the meaning of a text is whatever the reader gets out of it. This approach is sometimes known as *poststructuralism* (since it came after structuralism). Not only does it move away from authorial intention, it also goes beyond what the text says explicitly, finally asking, 'What effect does this passage have on me?' This fits nicely, of course, with postmodernism as a general philosophy, which is basically the view that there are no absolute standards – if it feels good do it, anything goes, and truth is whatever you make it. With poststructuralism, when it comes to interpretation, the bottom line – a fairly flexible one – is the reader's response to the passage.

Interestingly enough, this corresponds quite closely to the average small group Bible study which so often begins with those fateful words, 'Is anyone struck by anything in this passage?' The question focuses immediately on the reader's response. At times this can be helpful, especially if the point of the passage is to provoke you or make you change your attitude, as with the parables, for instance.

Consider the parable of the two sons in Luke chapter 15. Let's imagine two people: one is broke, drunk and a long way from home – we will call him Mr Smelly. The other is older, a respected Christian who enjoys his Sunday service as well as his Sunday lunch – he is Mr Comfortable. Now, if Mr Smelly could somehow hear Jesus' wonderful words across the centuries, he might well run to the arms of his Father in heaven and gratefully accept the offer of forgiveness for his sins. Then he is stuck with the task of finding a church that will be equally as forgiving. And, when Mr Smelly rolls up on Sunday morning, the parable goes to work on Mr Comfortable. What it most probably does is point an accusing finger at him for his unwillingness to embrace Mr Smelly, either literally or metaphorically, before hurrying home to his roast dinner.

So, what is the meaning of this parable? The meaning for Mr Comfortable is the accusing finger pointing in his direction. It is not an abstract meaning which he might enjoy discussing over lunch, especially if Mrs Comfortable, who remembers the parable only too well, invites Mr Smelly round for lunch that day. The meaning of the parable for her might be that she should break the habit of a lifetime and invite someone she didn't know to her house that afternoon. The parable has no meaning which can be separated off from the response it provokes. You can bet that the Comfortable family will not be having an abstract discussion about parable interpretation that evening. They will more likely be feeling the heat from the way that the parable has invaded their lives and changed them forever.

What of Mr Smelly? Well, what goes around comes around, and one day he may be comfortable too. Then who will he be lunching with? Once you have walked into its world, this parable will never let you go.

This example demonstrates that what the reader brings to the passage affects what he will take away from it, but this doesn't mean it is a free-for-all. As the old rhyme says, 'Wonderful things in the Bible I see, Most of them put there by you and by me.' Some readings are just plain wrong. You can probably easily think of examples, even examples where Christians have tried to use the Bible to justify appalling actions such as bombing civilians or abusive treatment of slaves, even apartheid.

Most cases, however, are not as clear cut as this. Does the Bible encourage wise financial investment or carefree giving with no worrying about tomorrow? The answer to this depends a bit on the kind of framework you bring to the Bible, or the kind of lifestyle or attitudes you have concerning money. Very likely there is more than one valid viewpoint. You may be the kind of person who needs to learn how to give, give, give – or perhaps you need to learn how to stop getting into debt. What the various Bible passages on this topic mean to you depends on who you are as a reader.

This is obviously not the same as saying that the meaning of a passage is whatever we make of it. A *deconstructionist* will try and tell you this: that the meaning is entirely up to the reader, and you can make any text mean the opposite of what it says. There is not a lot you can do when confronted with a paid-up deconstructionist, except buy them a drink and hope they will come back down to earth at some point.

You will by now have noted that hermeneutics can be daunting territory. In the light of this, the only sensible advice is to begin any observation with 'At the risk of oversimplification, I would say that...' Alternatively, pray for the gift of prophecy and try to cut your way through the hermeneutical hassle in one (inspired) stroke.

Crossing the bridge

Hearing God's communication is rather like any conversation where you both come with an agenda. You have things you want to talk about, God has things he wants to talk about, and at times it seems simply frustrating. However, developing the competence to be a good Bible reader involves learning both how to talk and how to listen. There are times when it is important to bring your frustrations and problems to your Bible reading and match them against the attitudes talked about in the passage, as with the parable of the two sons. You should expect the passage to 'speak to you'. At other times, it is good to learn how to listen so as to find out what is on God's agenda, which may be something you have never considered before.

The meaning of a Bible passage is not just pinned down to what it meant then or what it means to you now: it is an active thing which depends on you and God communicating together as you read. Sometimes you will discover that though you can get there from here, God may have in mind some altogether new place he wants you to be.

There are two things which kill off Bible reading. The first is not bothering to read it at all – a very quick way of losing interest in the Bible. The second is to read it assuming you already know what it is all about and not expecting to hear anything new. In between these two extremes is the chance to build the bridge between the world of the Bible and your own world, and to cross it.

12–09–823 BC 01:56 MT CARMEL   STOP PRESS TRANSMISSION P:06
COPY FOR TOMORROW'S EDITION OF ISRAEL TELEGRAPH
FROM OUR ROYAL CORRESPONDENT

FIRST RAIN FOR THREE YEARS
BAAL PROPHETS MASSACRED

Elijah the Prophet Returns in Mount Carmel Confrontation
 Astonishing scenes on Mount Carmel yesterday heralded
the return of the Yahweh prophet, Elijah, after several years in
the wilderness, and an extraordinary confrontation between
him and the prophets of Baal. King Ahab, who watched the
whole affair from the Royal Box, was on his way in the so-
called Ahab-mobile to Jezreel further inland, when thunderous
storms broke over the whole country, ending the three-year
drought which had so seriously threatened the land.

Elijah's challenge to the prophets of Baal to present themselves and call down fire from heaven was taken up in force,
and there were an estimated 400 of them yesterday on Mount
Carmel. But their sacrifices were to no apparent avail, until
Elijah intervened.

Fire From Sky

When Elijah stepped forward, there was a sudden release of
fire from the sky which burned up the sacrifice he had placed
on the altar at Mount Carmel.

Speculations about Elijah's motives are focusing on his long-
running dispute with royalty, and his well-known claim that
Yahweh, the God of Israel, is siding with the ordinary Israelite
and will not accept the royal abuse of privilege. Elijah's oppo-
sition to the ruling elite has had him in trouble before, notably
with Queen Jezebel.

An official statement from The Company of Prophets should
be released today, but a spokesperson said they did not wish
the public to think that their organisation was necessarily
committed to the line Elijah was taking. 'It's all very well for
him turning up after three years eating locusts somewhere in

the desert, but I think he's out of touch with the complex political realities of contemporary prophecy,' he said.

Rain details and weather forecast to follow. Other correspondents report the following headlines for tomorrow's editions:

> Elijah Wins Showdown of the Prophets as Rains Return
>   to Israel — *The Independent Israeli*
> Minister of Agriculture Quits — 'My faith in Baal was
>   Wrong' He Says — *The Israel Times*
> Shekel Crisis as Shock Rains Threaten Israel's
>   Membership of Single Near Eastern Currency — *The
>   Israeli Financial Times*
> Eli Shows 'Em! — *The Israel Sun*
> Burn Baby Burn — *The Israel Star*
> Is your god on the Loo? Asks Prophet — *The Israel Sport*

Chapter 5

THE SCIENCE AND ART OF HERMENEUTICS

The parable of the sausage-making machine and the art gallery

Hermeneutics: art or science?

For some people, producing interpretations of the Bible is a bit like making sausages. You take a large amount of meat, put it into your sausage-making machine and pull the right switches. Out come sausages in a user-friendly form. Likewise, you take a large amount of biblical text, put it into your hermeneutical machine and pull the right switches. Out come interpretations in a user-friendly form (often with three points all beginning with 'P'). Who you are doesn't make any difference: all you need is the ability to pull the switches.

Other people object to this. Competency to pull the switches isn't just a skill anyone can develop: it also involves who you are. In some ways, this goes back to our point about being sensitive to the passage, a good listener, and open to hearing unexpected and perhaps challenging points. So it makes a difference, according to this view, whether or not you are open to a spiritual relationship with God: because if you are not, then no amount of pulling the switches is going to enable you to hear God's voice emerge from your Bible study. People who argue this way see hermeneutics as more of an art than a science and interpreting a Bible passage as a bit like appreciating a painting.

Mysteriously, this parable of the sausage-making machine and the art gallery didn't make it into the canon. Experts are divided as to why this is so.

As is usually the case where two equal and opposite points both sound about right, the truth is more a case of 'both/and' rather than 'either/or'. The problems arise when people only see hermeneutics as mastering a set of methods that produce immediately obvious meanings which everyone can agree on. They will probably also see a relationship with God as simply something you bring to your Bible reading rather than something that can also grow out of your Bible reading.

The three easy steps to biblical interpretation?

So, focusing on methods can be good or bad. In practice, it fits well with an instant culture such as ours to have things set out in easy steps. Thus we have plenty of books with titles like 'The Seven Simple Steps to Making Your Church Grow' or 'Five Fast Steps to Powerful Prayer'; and now, of course, 'The Three Easy Steps to Biblical Interpretation'. (It is difficult, on the other hand, to imagine a best-selling title like 'A Hundred Hints for Hermeneutical Happiness'.)

One well-known approach to biblical interpretation is the three-step model: (1) observe what is in the text, (2) interpret it, (3) apply it. This, to use the image of the sausage-making machine, is the scientific approach that involves pulling certain switches in the right order and watching the 'meaning of the passage for today' drop out at the end of the process. This approach may be helpful, but it cannot be separated out into simple stages we must go through in order to interpret a passage correctly. Why not?

The problem is that there is so much to observe in any one passage. Unless you make some decisions about what you're looking for, you will never get started. Consider Acts 8:26–40, the wonderful story of Philip and the Ethiopian eunuch. A quick reading of the passage highlights the many points of interest which invite closer attention. Philip is ordered by an angel to intercept the eunuch, an important official in the Ethiopian court. The Ethiopian is on his way home after a trip to Jerusalem to worship. As he bowls along in his chariot, he is reading aloud from the book of Isaiah. Philip is instructed by the Holy Spirit to shadow the chariot closely. As he does so, the two strike up a conversation during which Philip asks the Ethiopian if he understands what he is reading. 'How can I', says the eunuch, 'when there's no one to explain it to me.' Philip proceeds to explain the passage and to expand it with the good news about Jesus. The Ethiopian is so overwhelmed that when he spies a pool of water by the road he demands to be baptised at once. Philip does so, and as soon as it is all over he is whisked away by the Spirit. Philip's sudden disappearance doesn't seem to worry the Ethiopian much and he goes on his way rejoicing.

Now you could go through this passage using the three-step approach, methodically making observations as to what it says or doesn't say. But suppose you wanted, for example, to see how much guidance the Holy Spirit gives Philip in this passage and then how much he just lets Philip get on with it. Unless you had decided beforehand that these things were what you wanted to know, would the 'observe and interpret' approach alone have prompted you to look for them? Probably not. Or to take another example, imagine being set the task of analysing a book like Ezekiel using the three-step method. Most likely your biggest complaint would be 'I don't know what I'm supposed to be looking for!' (Some people question whether Ezekiel himself had much of a clue.)

This 'knowing what to look for' stems from the more artistic side of hermeneutics. In practice, we get most of our ideas about what to look for from other people or from the books we read. Indeed, this is probably just as it should be – biblical interpretation happening in the company of the whole church, under the guidance of the Holy Spirit, in the context of learning from each other and not in an individualistic way.

The real benefit of something like the three-step method is more modest. It allows us to check on what we have done after we have done it. It tells us when our 'observations' are really just our interpretations: for example, in that account from Acts chapter 8, did we really observe the Spirit talking to Philip throughout or did we just assume that he continued to do so after the two dramatic commands we are told about? And there is nothing in this method to settle the question of how significant our observations might be. We cannot avoid having to use our own judgement at some point. (Just for the record, in Acts chapter 8, God most probably expects Philip to get on with talking to the Ethiopian and not wait for the Spirit to tell him what to do all the time. Or does he?)

DATE UNKNOWN   STOP PRESS TRANSMISSION
PLACE DIFFICULT TO PIN DOWN   P:07

'I CREATED WORLD' SAYS GOD

In a new, highly poetic introduction to his ongoing 'Holy Book' project, released today under the provisional title 'Genesis 1', God reveals one of his most startling claims yet: that he created the world. 'I was fed up with people worshipping all the stuff I made, like the sun and the moon and the sea and the land, as if they were gods, so I decided to set the record straight,' he said.

This latest revelation is bound to be controversial. Critics have been quick to point out that God's decision to use the imagery of 'six days of creation' lays him open to a somewhat literalistic interpretation. Others claim that the phrase 'male and female he created them' is a simple caving-in to feminist pressure in the wake of the controversy over the 'woman came from rib' theme in the famous Garden of Eden story.

But many were clearly very happy with the account. Yesterday an unidentified priestly source said, 'We all found the worship of creation very distressing. After all, no intelligent person goes around worshipping trees. We're very relieved to see a clear statement here that the sun should not be considered a god any longer.' However, it is doubtful whether the human willingness to worship created things will be dealt with quite so simply. Tree-worshipping communities were preparing counter-suits this morning.

A-ha!

Careful observation and interpretation will help us tune in to the wavelength of a passage. As we read and re-read the biblical text, we begin to bring it into focus. Finally, we become quite good at seeing it in its proper contexts and understanding what is and what is not significant. Each time you read the text, it changes who you are and teaches you more about what to look for. So when you come back to the passage again, it looks different and you are changed again. This is one reason why 'there is always something new in the Bible every time you read it'.

This process of you reading the text, the text changing you, and you reading the text again, is called 'going round the hermeneutical circle'. This may sound a bit too much like a vicious circle, so some people – observing that every time you go round the circle you learn more and improve your understanding of the passage – call it a *hermeneutical spiral*.

At some point, as you go up this spiral, you experience the a-ha! moment. This moment – impossible to describe but equally impossible to forget once you have experienced it – is when the Bible passage suddenly 'makes sense', 'falls into place', 'speaks to me' (depending on what kind of church you come from). It is much more difficult to have an a-ha! experience if you don't know what you're looking for, but it does happen.

Science and art

We have seen that the sausages we make with our hermeneutical science need supplementing with a more artistic outlook. When observing a painting, we don't go through a list of steps, eg (1) 'What colours are most prominent?', (2) 'What types of brush strokes are most in evidence?', (3) 'Are any of the images given prominence?' No, we stand back and get a feel for the whole work of art. Only then, in the light of the big picture, can we do the stuff about brushstrokes and colour tones. In the same way, we need to get a feel for the overall thrust of a Bible passage – for its basic ideas and teaching – before looking carefully at the details. There is no short cut to 'getting a feel for the Bible' except by reading and studying it regularly, and thinking creatively about what it says and how it says it. And keeping an eye out for those a-ha! moments.

The view from here

One question you may have at this point is 'It's all very well to say, "Think creatively", but how do you do this in practice? Do you simply sit around and wait for inspiration to strike?'

Of course, it is very helpful when inspiration does strike. But here is a hint for learning how to look at a Bible passage in a fresh way and how to get inside the way the characters work: try to see the story from someone else's point of view. Most biblical stories come with a point of view. The exodus, for example, is a great

---

AD 1515 02:11 WITTENBERG   STOP PRESS TRANSMISSION P:08

NEW INTERPRETATION OF ROMANS

Martin Luther, the 31-year old lecturer in Biblical Studies at the University of Wittenberg, has argued this week for a whole new approach to our understanding of Paul's letter to the Romans. Contrary to the standard idea that the righteousness of God revealed in the gospel is what condemns us because of our imperfection, Luther is arguing that the idea of God's righteousness is a positive one.

Although he has yet to publish his ideas, students this week were reporting that Luther saw God's righteousness as justifying us in spite of our sin. 'Justification by faith', he is said to have claimed, 'makes sense of Paul's letter to the Romans only if it means that God freely justifies sinners who do not deserve to be made righteous.'

That this is not the standard position of the church hardly needs emphasising. A spokesperson for the church suggested that talk of the reformation of official church teaching was premature. 'I'm sure it will all blow over,' he said.

---

moment for the Jews, but not for the Egyptians. Not that we are going to suggest much sympathy for the Egyptians, but it will help us get under the skin of the story to rewrite it from their perspective. We did that with this very example in an earlier part of the book.

The technical name for reading a passage this way is 'reading against the grain'. Fortunately, you don't need to know that.

AROUND THE TIME OF ABRAHAM   STOP PRESS TRANSMISSION
02:17 THE VALLEY OF SIDDIM   P:09

POLICE ID SUSPECTS FOR
SODOM AND GOMORRAH BOMBING

Further to the devastation of the cities of Sodom and Gomorrah reported earlier, police have issued profiles of two men they wish to question. They were last seen drinking cappuccinos late Monday afternoon at the roadside diner out near Zoar.

The diner's owner reported that the taller of the two had seemed especially irritable. He had looked distracted and preoccupied, and had complained bitterly about the phone system being down again. He had wanted to contact someone called Lot, but was unable to get through. The shorter one was slightly overweight and had spent his whole time poring over passports which, it is now known, were fakes used to gain entry to the city. Both men had talked about a third member of the party, who had apparently stayed behind at Mamre and had been seen talking to Abraham.

Lot is presumed dead in the aftermath of the bombing. Police are still wanting to contact Abraham. Motives for the attack remain unclear, but police said today that the explosive used in the blasts was extraordinarily powerful and had left virtually no traces of where it might be from. The search for survivors goes on, but a police spokesperson said, 'It would be a miracle if anybody survived this.'

Chapter 6

PUTTING IT ALL TOGETHER
Hermeneutical hints
from Psalm 1

We have come a long way from our original questions about how to get at the true meaning of 'what the Bible says to me'. So, in the shade of the tree that dominates Psalm 1, it is time to conclude with an example of how we might bring together some of the things we been looking at by actually interpreting a biblical passage, one that is about living happily, and hermeneutically, ever after.

The tree by the river
    1 Happy are those
        who do not follow the advice of the wicked,
    or take the path that sinners tread,
        or sit in the seat of scoffers...

Psalm 1 opens with a description of a happy person. The theme of the Psalm is 'how to be happy'. (Actually, in some translations the word is 'blessed', which has the advantage of sounding much more religious but the disadvantage of not meaning much to most people.) The happy person is the one who doesn't let his life become dominated by the wicked, the one whose agenda isn't set by the 'sinners' he mixes with. His agenda is set somewhere else.

    2 but their delight is in the law of the Lord,
        and on his law they meditate day and night.

His agenda, we discover, is set by meditating on the 'law' day and night. The Hebrew word for 'law' is *torah*. 'Torah' is the name for the first five books of the Bible (the Pentateuch) and includes the law of Moses on which Israel based its daily living. So, verse 2 is saying, 'the Torah is what it's all about if you want to get happy.'

Now this could easily come across as a bit depressing. In fact you can already hear the preacher gearing himself up for the awful conclusion: just read your Bible every morning and every night and you too can live happily ever after! But we should be suspicious of this claim, because (1) it is not what the verse says, since it doesn't mention either 'reading' or 'the Bible', and (2) it is a psalm, not a legal code, and is therefore more likely trying to paint us a picture than lay down a law. The picture comes in verse 3:

> 3 They are like trees
>   planted by streams of water,
> which yield their fruit in its season,
>   and their leaves do not wither.
> In all that they do, they prosper.

The image is of someone who is like a tree beside a river whose roots reach deep down into the watered soil and whose fruit appears in due season. This, apparently, is what it is like to meditate on the Torah.

If we go straight for our scientific hermeneutical approach, we may be led astray, concluding that the application of this is that we should read the Bible every day and thus be happy. This is fair enough as far as it goes, especially if we accept that the last verse of the psalm gives us a rough idea of what it means by happiness:

> 6 for the Lord watches over the way of the righteous,
>   but the way of the wicked will perish.

But the power of this tree-by-the-river image will (surprise, surprise) only come by meditating, or at least reflecting, on it – rather as the psalm itself suggests. If you think about this psalm, let its image become part of your thinking and really get inside it, then – a-ha! – the text will seize you. And once it has done that, it will never let you go. But if it doesn't grab you, then you can read

Psalm 1 as often as you like and it will never be much more than a nice little poem at the beginning of Psalms.

Hermeneutics with roots

The next obvious question is not 'What can I observe in the text?' but, rather, 'What kind of a-ha! moment am I looking for?' What is the clue to the big picture this psalm is painting?

The clue is not in how often you read the Torah, or how well you avoid the advice of sinners: the clue is in the roots of the tree. If you start from the roots and work upwards, the rest of the psalm will fall into place. A-ha! It is all about hermeneutics with roots.

If the tree is healthy and its roots are well-nourished, it will produce fruit and it will produce it in season. There are no short cuts and no tricks the tree can use to produce extra fruit on demand. Compare this with someone whose approach to the Bible is 'I need God's help to make this decision about my job/buying a car/who to marry…, so I'll spend a day praying and reading the Bible and ask for God's help'. What kind of tree would this be? One which dumps a whole load of water on its roots in the hope of producing fruit in double-quick time. But, of course, producing fruit doesn't work that way. You can't shower the tree's roots the day before the harvest and expect it to make a difference. In the same way, someone whose biblical roots are firmly established and well looked after can be confident about making decisions, because to them God's promise is that the right outcome will come at the right time.

Spirituality, says this psalm, is a matter of looking after your roots. This may or may not mean a Bible reading every morning and evening, but it does mean doing whatever it takes to keep your biblical roots in good shape. What this means in practice will depend to some extent on you, the reader: but whatever it means it is important that you do it, because it is basically about your spiritual health.

Hark, I hear the canon!

What of the context of the passage? Well, we don't know much about its historical context. Its literary context helped us to recognise that this poem is not a law for us to obey. However, the most important context in this case is the canonical context, or where it is placed in the finished Bible.

Psalm 1 is deliberately placed at the beginning of the book of Psalms as a kind of introduction on how to use the rest of the book. Christians down through the centuries have often found the psalms to be great resources for meditation. This, we now see, is not because they give you applications to work on but because they provide nourishing soil for your roots, which changes who you are (and thus propels you on to the hermeneutical spiral in a positive upwards direction).

The significance of the canonical (biblical) context goes even further. When the Jews organised their Bible, they didn't do it in the same order as the Christians organised their Old Testament, even though it contains basically the same books. The Jews put it in three parts: the Torah (Genesis–Deuteronomy, the 'five books of Moses'); the Prophets (which included most of what we call the histories!); the Writings (everything that didn't qualify for the other two sections). The Torah was the foundation of the whole Jewish scriptures; the Prophets began with the book of Joshua; and the Writings began with the book of Psalms.

Now in Joshua chapter 1, Joshua is commissioned by God after Moses' death. And what does God say to Joshua? In verse 8, he says, 'This book of the torah shall not depart out of your mouth; you shall meditate on it day and night.' Now where have we heard that before? Right back in Psalm 1. So what we find is that both the other sections of the Jewish scriptures start with a reminder to meditate daily on the Torah. It is difficult to imagine a more scripture-centred approach to the idea of living a life to please God.

Hermeneutics in an instant society

Psalm 1, therefore, pulls together a lot of the things we have thought about. It suggests a way we can be changed as people. It gives us a picture of learning to think biblically. And, as we are changed, our meditation on the Bible will continue to nourish us, helping us go round and up the hermeneutical spiral – in other words, we keep on getting more and more out of our Bible reading.

Our ability to understand the Bible is all part of our spiritual growth and our relationship with God. This is so different from the attitude of our 'slot-machine', instant culture which likes everything, including the spiritual life, to be programmable and to offer instant results; which likes a nice methodology that allows you to put the Bible passage in at one end and get a handy interpretation, complete with practical applications, at the other. It would rather that 'Being an Expert in Interpreting the Bible' were just a series of steps you go through to get blessed.

This doesn't seem to be what 'being biblical' is all about when you come back to the Bible itself. Instead it invites us into a life-long process of change and growth. We put our spiritual roots deep into biblical soil and entrust ourselves to God to see where our faithful interpretation will take us. And that's hermeneutics, folks!

GLOSSARY

For the would-be expert who has no time to read entire books, just memorise one definition a day to stay ahead. Some of these we covered in the book, some we didn't, but they are all something to do with the science, and art, of interpretation.

Allegory

The idea that a story about one thing is really a coded way of talking about another, eg Jesus tells a story of different seeds and soils in Matthew 13 but he is really talking about how people respond to God. Reading the Bible as allegory is very handy whenever it seems to be talking about rape, murder, holy war or some other 'noble' human activity – which it does embarrassingly often.

Authorial intention

The authorial intention of a passage is whatever the author intended to say, except in the case of Jude 3 where the author tells us that he has not said what he intended to say but has written about something else instead.

Authority

The authority of a book always depends on the author. Since, in the case of the Bible, God is the author, it is a good idea to do what the Bible says.

Biblical interpretation

The process (science, or art) of understanding the Bible. This is not exactly the same as hermeneutics, which is really a broader word referring to the whole question of how we can decide what makes an interpretation a good one or a bad one. But, in general, you can get away with confusing the two terms as long as you speak confidently enough. Which, of course, is what has happened in this book.

Clarity of scripture

Surprisingly, not the idea that everything the Bible says is clear. Rather, it is the view that enough biblical teaching is clear and straightforward for us to live our lives faithfully in the light of

God's word. It was developed during the Reformation in response to the assertion that only experts could interpret the Bible. Given this, it is hard to explain how reformers like Luther or Calvin managed to find all sorts of passages which, they claimed, were 'clearly' about the awfulness of the Pope.

Contextualisation

The theory that the Bible comes to us out of a particular culture and needs to be translated into terms which make sense in today's cultures. Thus, in a culture where houses are built on sticks to avoid flood water, Jesus' parable about the wise and foolish builder tells the story of the wise man who built his house on sticks. It gets more complicated when you then have Jesus saying to Peter, 'Upon this stick I will build my church.'

Eisegesis

A made-up word designed to contrast with *exegesis*. To accuse someone of *eisegesis* is to charge them with the horrendous crime of reading into a text something which isn't there. Eisegesis is very common in *proof-texting*. In fact, it is just very common.

Exegesis

From the Greek meaning to lead (*gere*) out of (*ex-*), hence the process of drawing out (or reading out) the meaning of the text.

Feminist hermeneutics

Feminist hermeneutics interprets the Bible with the working assumption that at least some of the things the Bible says about women were just part of the presuppositions of the ancient culture the Bible came from, and are not what God was revealing. This includes such striking biblical observations as women being the weaker sex and wives being told to obey their husbands, as well as not having authority over men. Opponents of this approach say that it makes the Bible totally subjective because you can then disregard whatever bits you don't like. Defenders point out that we have already taken this approach with issues like slavery. In fact the issue is not whether the approach is subjective, because every interpretation is subjective, but whether the particular opinions involved are good ones. This is a much more tricky issue, so it doesn't get discussed as often.

Four-fold meaning of scripture

In the Middle Ages, it was common to argue that there were four levels of meaning in any passage: (1) the literal meaning (what the text meant in its historical context); (2) the allegorical meaning (what it referred to in the grand scheme of Christian doctrine if interpreted symbolically); (3) the moral meaning (interpreting any passage for the individual in terms of what it could say about daily living); and (4) the obscure anagogical, or mystagogical, meaning (relating whatever is left out by the other three to the future).

Under this scheme, 'Jerusalem' meant (1) the literal city of Jerusalem; (2) the church; (3) the individual soul; and (4) the heavenly city to come. It was a bit harder to say what, for instance, Zechariah's two olive trees stood for (Zechariah 4:3–5); but then not even the angel who showed them to him knew that, so perhaps it is an unfair example.

Fundamentalist

Anyone more conservative in their interpretations than you are is a fundamentalist. (See also *liberal*.)

Hermeneut

This delightful, although increasingly unfashionable, word simply means 'one who does hermeneutics'. It can therefore mean 'interpreter' or 'exegete' or any of the other things we do when we are working on the Bible. 'Although I am an inexperienced hermeneut...' will dazzle your audience long enough for you to get away with whatever outrageous point it was you wanted to make.

Hermeneutical circle

See *hermeneutical spiral*.

Hermeneutical spiral

See *hermeneutical circle*.

Hermeneutics

What this book is about. (Do *not* see *biblical interpretation*.)

Illumination

After inspiring the Bible, the Holy Spirit has not decided to move on to more general miracle-working and prophetic ministries and leave the Bible to take care of itself. Instead, he continues to shed light on what he has inspired. This is what is known as *illumination*.

Inspiration

Belief in the inspiration of the Bible does not refer to the fact that it is full of really inspired ideas, but rather to the notion that the biblical text is 'God-breathed', ie is exactly as God wanted it. The word 'inspiration' is used in 2 Timothy 3:16, where it could indeed be translated as 'God-breathed'. (See also *illumination*.)

Liberal

Anyone less conservative in their interpretations than you are is a liberal. (See also *fundamentalist*.)

Perspiration

After considering the God-breathed aspect of Scripture (see also *inspiration*), many find that the rest of interpretation becomes sheer hard work. The technical term for this is *perspiration*.

Presuppositions

The ideas and beliefs you bring to a text whenever you read. You may be aware of them (eg 'I'm going to believe this book, whatever it tells me') or you may be unaware of them (eg 'Jesus was a nice white man who was really a Jolly Decent Englishman'). Hermeneutics helps us adjust our presuppositions to get them in line with the text.

Proof-texting

Using a Bible verse or passage out of context to provide a handy 'proof' of whatever point you are trying to make, regardless of what the Bible verse you used is actually trying to talk about. Proof-texting is extremely popular because it is much easier than interpreting the Bible properly.

Translations

Since the Bible was written in Hebrew and Greek (and even a little bit of Aramaic), it is highly recommended that you read it in a translation. For a long time the King James Version (KJV), produced in 1611, has been the major English translation. However, the language in that version is now pretty dated and, although it is called the 'Authorised Version', this only means that it was authorised by King James, not by God. More recent translations, often based on a better understanding of the Hebrew and Greek, can cut out a lot of mistaken interpretations, eg when the KJV talks about the friends of the paralysed man not being able to get near Jesus because of the press (Mark 2:4).

Truth
Truth is much easier to recognise than to define. As a good rule of thumb, if it is in the Bible then it is true, but the reverse does not hold. For example, it is true that a lot of Christians voted for Margaret Thatcher, but it would be difficult to relate this to the Bible.

Typology
(1) The view that Old Testament things or events 'stand for' later things or events and reveal truths about them ahead of time. Paul, for instance, interprets the rock in the wilderness as Christ (1 Corinthians 10:4), and sees an old law about muzzling the ox as a principle relevant to the question of whether apostles should be paid for their work (1 Corinthians 9:9), which perhaps suggests that he had an interesting self-image. (2) The study of which fonts the Bible was produced in.

Weather
When Ezra read from the book of the law (Ezra 10:9), the two things that distressed the crowds were (1) the realisation that they had sinned against God and (2) the heavy rain. The role of the weather in our understanding of the Bible remains a vastly under-explored subject.

Zwingli
A Swiss reformer, who had hardly any new ideas on hermeneutics, but whose name somehow always seems to be the last word on any subject.

FURTHER READING

The problem for any book on biblical interpretation is how to spend time both clarifying and interpreting the biblical text as well as explaining why and how the various hermeneutical approaches work. Here, of course, we have done nothing but skim the surface of these issues, providing a few pointers along the way in between trying to show that a lot of the jargon and concepts are nothing to be afraid of. But if you want to get down to some serious interpretation, where do you go next? The best basic book for taking you through the different approaches needed for the various biblical genres is:

> Stephen Motyer, *The Bible with Pleasure: How to get the most out of reading your Bible*, Crossway Books, 1997.

Doing the same thing, but in more detail and with longer examples, is:

> Gordon D Fee and Douglas Stuart, *How to Read the Bible for All its Worth* (2nd edn), Scripture Union, 1993.

If you really like this approach and want the whole works in one volume, including a massive list of further reading for almost any subject you want to explore, then go for:

> William W Klein, Craig L Blomberg and Robert L Hubbard, *Introduction to Biblical Interpretation*, Word (US), 1993.

A very helpful introduction to the more general issues of hermeneutics is provided by:

> Moisés Silva, *Has the church misread the Bible? The history of interpretation in the light of current issues*, Apollos, 1987.

This is the first of seven volumes in a series called 'Foundations of Contemporary Interpretation'. The other six follow it up with more detailed studies of different areas of hermeneutics, such as linguistic, literary or historical approaches. Great for enthusiasts, but not bed-time reading.

Finally, for the more adventurous reader, a good book on how to approach Bible study creatively, with some interesting ideas for being changed through your Bible reading, is:

Walter Wink, *Transforming Bible Study* (2nd edn), Mowbray (an imprint of Cassell plc), 1990.